THE FEARLESS FACTOR

HOW TO OVERCOME FEAR AND TURN YOUR DREAM INTO REALITY

Isaac Maxwell

Introduction

Nobody is brave by nature. We cannot, however, continue to live in dread. Living a brave life is one of the finest ways to achieve success in both our personal and professional lives because we can't let fear determine what we should do when we should do it, and how we should do it. Fear will always prevent us from obtaining what we deserve and what we desire, therefore we must prevent that from happening.

It may indeed seem like "it's easier said than done" but it doesn't change the truth that living a bold life and being fearless is very much feasible. Undoubtedly, it is humane to feel dread, but with that fear also comes the choice to act coolly and bravely. We must learn to overcome our fear if we are to live the lives we want.

We all have moments of terror, and every one of us experiences fear for a different reason. For instance, one person can be fearful to introduce themselves to someone they respect, another might be worried to borrow money to expand their company, and still, another would be afraid to confront someone. The fact that we all sometimes feel dread is well acknowledged. The majority of us, however, are unaware of the chances that our times of terror provide since they have the potential to enrich our lives with the valuable, brave power that they help us cultivate via the special chance they present.

Popular positive thinker Dale Carnegie famously remarked that facing your fears head-on is the fastest way to overcome them. Contrarily, Aristotle elaborated on this phrase in one of his quotations by stating that because bravery is the first of human qualities, it opens the door for the possibility of subsequent virtues.

How can I really turn my fear into confidence is undoubtedly the thought that is nagging in the back of your mind right now. Actually, you don't need to worry about that anymore since this book is supposed to lay out the actions you may take to overcome fear and lead the life you desire. It takes you on an exciting trip to learn how to develop your sense of self-worth and confidence, quiet your inner critic, and mute negativity. Your boldest aspirations will come true as you gain confidence and bravery. Therefore, buckle up while we enjoy the trip together.

How can I quickly turn my [illegible] into [illegible]... [illegible] the thought that is nagging in the back of your mind right now. Also, you don't need to worry about that anymore since this book is supposed to lay [illegible] [illegible] [illegible] [illegible] [illegible] [illegible] [illegible] [illegible] [illegible] [illegible] [illegible] [illegible] [illegible] together.

Chapter 1: Definition, Signs, and Causes of Fear

What is fear?

Fear may alert us to the possibility of injury or the actuality of danger, whether it be psychological or physical. Both a strong personal emotional reaction and a universal physiological reaction are present in fear. Humans naturally experience fear, which is a primal, strong feeling. While fear may be a sign of mental health issues such as post-traumatic stress disorder, phobias, social anxiety disorder, and panic disorder, it can also be the result of imagined threats, though this is frequently the case.

However, keep in mind that highly individualized dread is a result of an emotional reaction, and on the other hand, our body also reacts in certain ways when we sense danger — this is a physiological reaction. High amounts of adrenaline, a racing heartbeat, and perspiration are a few of the physical responses to fear, which is a normal feeling and a survival strategy.

Symptoms

You may respond to fear physically, emotionally, or even both, as was already said. While it's probable that every one of us may respond to dread differently, the following are some typical signs of fear:

- Nausea
- Dry mouth
- Chills
- shortness of breath
- Rapid heartbeat

- Trembling
- Upset stomach
- chest discomfort

Psychological symptoms like a sense of impending death, being out of control, being angry, or feeling overwhelmed can also occur in some people.

Causes

The majority of people don't understand how complicated fear is. Even the strongest person on the planet experiences fear; despite what some people may say, who says that fear is only for the weak? The world's best boxer or wrestler comes to mind. Do you think someone like that would be afraid? Evidently, the things we dread change from person to person, and what makes one person scared may be more or less complicated than what makes another person fearful.

Nevertheless, the following are some typical fear triggers:

- Real environmental threats
- Imagined occurrences
- Future events
- The unknown
- Situations or specific items (such as flying, heights, crowds, roaches, snakes, and spiders), among others.

Be aware that certain phobias may be linked to painful memories or connections. Others that help survive may be impacted by evolution since they often come naturally.

Types

Here are some of the several types of anxiety disorders, which are all marked by fear:

- Specific phobia
- Generalized anxiety disorder
- Post-traumatic stress disorder (PTSD)
- Separation anxiety disorder
- Social anxiety disorder
- Specific phobia
- Fear of heights
- Panic disorder

Why You Need to Face Your Fear

The majority of people only experience mental forms of fear, some of which include the following: fear of being hurt, fear of being alone, fear of aging, fear of humiliation, fear of rejection, fear of judgment, fear of change, fear of failure, fear of losing out, fear of authority, fear of strangers, fear of people, fear of public speaking, and the list goes on.

When you consider your future, do you get a feverish feeling because you're unsure of what lies ahead? Are you easily intimidated or do you experience frequent fear? Here are some justifications for why you should steel yourself to face your anxieties if you think you lack bravery.

1. **Your potential is restricted by fear**: You find it difficult to develop and advance in life when you are afraid. Living your best life and improving yourself become quite difficult when you're motivated by fear, and you'll find it very difficult to believe in personal development. It is hard to reach higher states of awareness if we continue to live in a country of fear. We must not be trapped in fear if we are to reach the higher states of enlightenment, peace, joy, love, and acceptance.

One of the biggest issues in our modern culture is that most of us tend to vibrate at a continuous level of dread. In order for us to realize our full potential, we must prevent fear from taking over our lives. If fear is the sole factor influencing our actions, emotions, and ideas, we will be reduced to becoming its slaves. Recognize that if you keep behaving out of fear, you will never realize your full potential.

2. **You can never really escape fear**: How much time can you spend avoiding your fear? Consider it for yourself. What has running done to you since you began to do it? Has it helped you entirely overcome your phobia, or does it only make things more difficult? Running will just give you a false sense of security, but if you allow your fear to control you and refuse to confront it, it will infiltrate everything you do. Fear in the mind is all-pervasive. Even while it may not be immediately apparent, you cannot completely escape dread. Keep in mind that as you run, fear will always try to catch up with you more. Eventually, fear will corner you, leaving you with no way out.

You'll only have two choices when this eventually happens: brace yourself to face your fear or tremble violently. You would realize that learning to overcome fear now is crucial because avoiding difficult situations is never the best course of action. No matter what you are afraid of, convince yourself that now is the moment to face it.

3. **Your energy is wasted on fear**: When you give in to fear, you're using your energy in an unproductive way. Fear drains your physical and mental resources and pulls you back instead of allowing you to brainstorm, identify solutions, plan a course of action, and calmly assess the situation. Even though fear, particularly for adrenaline junkies, may sometimes be a motivating element to do more and perform better, it can also be a waste of emotional and mental energy.

4. **All of your fear is mental**. Funny how fear, despite frequently appearing threatening and frightening, is harmless. Mental fear is based on the imagined threat that you have created. An excellent illustration of this is the widespread fear of speaking in front of groups of people. Do you ever consider the reasons behind people's intense aversion to public speaking? Speaking in front of an audience won't really hurt your physical health in any way. You'll eventually understand, though, that this fear arises from your worry that you might make a mistake, look foolish, offend someone, or blunder. You see, you create all of these anxieties in your head. All of your fears—whether you believe the audience won't be interested in listening to your speech, the presentation will go wrong, you'll forget what you were going to say, or anything else—are unfounded since they haven't yet occurred.

Even though they have previously occurred in the past, there is no assurance that any of these events will occur in the future. It is up to you to bring about any result you choose. The future is still in the future. You're in the here and now. Unwind and perform well to make a difference.

Chapter 2: Five things about Fear you probably didn't know.

Understanding the science of fear is necessary for you to learn how to overcome your fears and transform them into courage. This brings us to the next five facts about the fear that you probably didn't know. Have you ever questioned why some people enjoy being afraid while others avoid it while enjoying scary movies and roller coasters? Here are some things to remember regarding fear.

Fear is physical

You should already be aware of this as it was previously established that fear may cause a physiological response. Fear not only makes you physically react strongly, but it also makes you mentally react similarly. When you experience fear, your body begins to respond. Your blood flow will change, you'll start breathing more quickly, your heart rate and blood pressure will rise, stress hormones like adrenaline and cortisol will be released, and your nervous system will become alert as your amygdala gets to work. Due to changes in blood flow, your body also gets ready for fight or flight, making it simple for you to start punching or running for your life.

Fear can cloud your judgment.

Yes, fear may cause confusion. The word "foggy" simply means to be "befuddled" or "confused," in case you're not quite sure what the term implies. If you like watching movies, you would know exactly what this is about. For illustration, imagine that a man was getting "cozy" with his girlfriend when three armed men barged in. You might see how baffled or confused he would be if that man were gripped by dread.

He won't be able to think properly at that time, and he'll be so melted that his ability to make decisions will decrease. Some areas of the brain cease functioning when fear occurs, while other sections of the brain become very active. The cerebral cortex, the part of the brain in charge of judgment and logic, is impaired when fear takes hold of your body.

Fear may turn into pleasure.

Do you ever wonder why certain people like being caught up in stressful or frightful situations? People who enjoy scary movies, haunted houses, and rollercoasters thrive on the anxiety they experience. For these people, the thrills continue long after the activity has ended because the excitation transfer process causes their brain and body to remain stimulated. During a manufactured terror encounter, more of the neurotransmitter dopamine is created, which induces pleasure.

Phobia is not fear.

Many people tend to confuse phobia with fear without realizing that they are very different emotions. For instance, if the thought of lying on the beach makes you feel helpless, traumatized, and terrorized, you may be going beyond just being afraid. On the other hand, you could merely wish to stay away from swimming in the water as a result of a recent movie you saw. Phobia, to put it simply, is a more advanced kind of dread. A phobia is stronger than fear. If you find yourself going to great lengths to avoid things like rodents, roaches, people, spiders, elevators, or water, you may have a phobia. Fear turns into a phobia when it becomes impossible for you to maintain a constant quality of life and when it interferes with your capacity to perform. Fears are normal responses people have to things or situations.

Fear protects you

Yes, it was quite apparent when it was written; that fear does keep you safe. Contrary to what you may have thought, heard, or believed, fear protects us and it is imperative that we feel it. We all feel fear, a biological and normal state, and although it may have harmful effects, it can also be beneficial and healthy since fear is a complex human emotion.

Chapter 3: Common and Strange Fears

The term "phobia" derives from the Greek word "Phobos," which means terror or dread. A phobia is only an illogical dread of anything, and it is unlikely to damage anybody. Phobias sometimes entail fears related to certain circumstances, medical conditions, natural surroundings, or animals, among other things. Phobias may more specifically be defined as an irrational, acute, and enduring dread of a certain scenario or item. Certain situations and things are associated with distinct phobias.

Phobias may affect a person's ability to function well in the classroom, at work, and in daily life at home. They are significantly different from ordinary anxieties and may also result in substantial discomfort. People who have a phobia about something usually manage to tolerate it while experiencing extreme worry or terror, or they may try to avoid it. However, keep in mind that there are an infinite number of scenarios and items, therefore the list of particular phobias is pretty vast. According to some experts, phobias exist in all different sizes and forms, and there are five main categories into which particular phobias usually fall:

- Fears related to certain circumstances (driving, using an elevator, or flying);
- Fears related to the natural environment (darkness, sun, mountains, thunder, heights)
- Fears related to medical conditions, injury, or blood (falls, shattered bones, injection)
- Fears related to animals (such as those of insects, cats, dogs, bunnies, and spiders)

- Others (drowning, loud noises, choking)

These categories may be used to describe an infinite number of particular things and circumstances.

Common Phobias

The list is infinite when it comes to phobias. However, it seems that phobias never go away since researchers and medical professionals often uncover new phobias. These medical professionals have been compelled to up to the challenge of labeling such phobias as they are discovered. To do this, they create a moniker using the -phobia suffix and a relevant Latin or Greek prefix linked to the fear. For instance, the word hydrophobia, which denotes a fear of water, is created by combining the words hydro (water) and phobia (fear). Additionally, there is phobophobia, also known as the fear of all fear.

However, when it comes to common phobias, there is a source that lists some of the most prevalent phobias. This source was published in the British Journal of Psychiatry and was based on a 1998 study that included more than 8,000 participants.

These are them:

- **Zoophobia**, the fear of animals
- **Ophiophobia**, the fear of snakes
- **Hydrophobia**, the fear of water
- **Hemophobia**, the fear of blood
- **Autophobia** is the fear of being alone
- **Astraphobia**, the fear of thunder and lightning
- **Arachnophobia**, the fear of spiders

- **Aerophobia**, the fear of flying
- **Acrophobia**, the fear of heights

Special Phobias

You shouldn't be shocked to learn that we have distinct phobias in addition to our typical fears. Because most sufferers of these phobias don't reveal their odd worries to their physicians, which makes them challenging to diagnose, and because some of these phobias may only afflict a small number of individuals at a time, we refer to them as unique phobias.

Dealing with Phobia

Simply said, a mix of drugs and counseling is what is used to treat phobias, thus the ideal person to talk to if you seek treatment for your fear is a licensed mental health professional or a psychologist. However, a kind of psychotherapy known as exposure treatment is well known for being particularly successful in curing some phobias. Working with your psychologist during exposure treatment will provide you the opportunity to learn how to become less sensitive to whatever gives you anxiety.

With the help of this therapy, you'll be able to learn to manage your responses and receive the chance to alter how you feel or think about the circumstance or item. Some of the drugs that may be prescribed to you to assist lessen your panic, fear, worry, and any other uneasy sensations you may have include benzodiazepines and beta-blockers. These drugs are really effective at making exposure therapy less upsetting, but keep in mind that they aren't really a way to cure phobias; rather, they're only meant to get you through exposure therapy.

Chapter 4: Increasing Your Self-Respect and Confidence

If you have a healthy amount of self-confidence, you have a good chance of succeeding in both your career and personal life. The degree of faith you have in your judgment, traits, and talents is described as self-confidence, which is noted to be essential for your health and psychological well-being.

Just as you must have a healthy amount of self-confidence, it's also essential that you work on your self-esteem since, in the absence of doing so, it will lead you to get enmeshed in falsely destructive ideas. The view and impression we have of ourselves as well as how we feel about ourselves are both components of self-esteem.

Why Do People Feel Low About Their Selves?

There are many different causes of low self-esteem in people. You have a significant likelihood of having poor self-esteem if you frequently believed as a child that you couldn't live up to standards and that perception carried over into your adult life. You could have some problems as a result of this mindset in your professional and interpersonal relationships. If you're going through a bereavement, divorce, or any other traumatic life event, your self-esteem may also take a hit.

Benefits of self-Confidence

When you prepare yourself to work on your self-confidence, there are many scrumptious advantages waiting for you. Here are some of them.

- **Better performance**: You have a greater probability of doing better work when you feel confident. On the other side, if you constantly think that you're not good enough, you won't be able to put your energy into your efforts and everything you do will feel like a waste of time and effort.
- **Healthy relationships:** Self-confidence increases self-love and understanding of others. It also increases self-love. Additionally, having self-confidence makes it easier for you to end unhealthy, taxing, and unworthy relationships.

- **Willingness to attempt new things:** Whether you're enrolling in a cooking class or applying for a job, you'll find it much simpler to put yourself out there when you have confidence in who you are and what you can accomplish. When you have confidence in yourself, you'll be eager to attempt new things and be interested in them.

- **Resilience:** As we go through life, we will undoubtedly encounter certain difficulties and problems, and the degree to which we are able to overcome them depends on our resilience. When you have confidence in yourself, you may really improve your resilience.

How to Increase Your Self-confidence

- **Never evaluate yourself against others.** Comparisons are unhealthy; doing so will do you more damage than good. For example, comparing your wealth to that of your friends or your appearance to that of your Facebook pals is unhealthy. It is not your obligation to concentrate on other people's life. Think about your life. Keep a daily notebook of your appreciation. Whenever you feel jealous of someone else's life, always remind yourself of your own accomplishments and qualities.

- **Be in the company of uplifting individuals.** You may want to give yourself some time to carefully consider your surroundings. Do these individuals accept you for who you are, or do they judge you frequently? Do they like making you feel inferior or do they enjoy making you feel superior? You should surround yourself with people who care about you and want the best for you because the people you spend time with may have an impact on your attitudes and how you feel about yourself.

- **Take good care of your body.** When you use self-care to engage your mind, body, and spirit in something constructive, you'll inevitably feel more confident. But it's hard to feel good about yourself if you're mistreating your body. Regular sleep, meditation, exercise, and healthy food are a few self-care techniques that may help you increase your self-confidence.

- **Be nice to yourself.** Be less harsh with yourself. Be nice to yourself because, no matter what occurs in life, you'll come to know that you're your only resource. Remember to be gentle to yourself if you have a setback, miss, fail, or make a mistake.

- **Engage in positive self-talk.** When you engage in negative self-talk, your confidence may be lowered and your potential may be constrained. On the other side, when you employ upbeat and encouraging self-talk, you'll feel encouraged to take on fresh tasks, get through self-doubt, and cultivate self-compassion. Therefore, anytime you make a mistake, be sure to remind yourself that "I can do nothing right" rather than "at least I learned something" or "I can do better next time."

- **Face your phobias**. This is the whole subject of the book. You'll feel refueled and more motivated to face your worries after making connections and putting everything together. Building your confidence by facing your worries head-on is a terrific approach to do so. The main reason why most individuals dread so much is that they lack confidence, however by facing your fears and doing tough tasks, you can build your confidence.

Simple Techniques to Increase Self-Esteem

1. Develop a new talent. When you improve at something that aligns with your skills and interests, your competence grows. Your self-esteem will get an additional boost.

2. Make a list of your achievements. List your successes, no matter how little they may have been. They should include all you do each week as well as all of your self-proud actions. Review this list whenever you need to do anything and are feeling down.

3. Use your imagination. Take a dancing lesson, register for a neighborhood theater play, compose a short story or poem, or bust out your old instrument. When you are engaged in creative activities, your brain is stimulated, and you might regain your sense of flow in life.

4. Become very clear about your values. Knowing what you stand for can boost your confidence. Determine your values and give them a thorough examination.

5. Examine your limiting assumptions. False ideas will constantly want to take over your head and confine you, but don't let them flourish. If you ever catch yourself thinking poorly of yourself, stop and set a goal for yourself.

6. Keep your feet just outside of your comfort zone. Your confidence starts at the outside limit of your comfort zone. Try something new, meet new people, approach an issue in an unexpected manner, or do anything else that will make you feel a little uncomfortable. Stretch yourself by going outside your comfort zone.

7. Be of assistance. Give someone what you are good at doing as a present. You may provide someone direct assistance, share useful resources with them, or teach them something they wish to learn. Utilize your talents, skills, and abilities to assist others.

8. Forgive your past. When you choose to repair the past by enlisting the help of a qualified counselor, it may be simple to go into the future with confidence. However, if you allow unsolved problems and drama to weigh you down, you risk becoming stuck in poor self-esteem.

9. Give up worrying about what other people may think. When all you care about is what others will think of you, you'll never be free to be who you are. See, no matter how great you strive to look in their eyes, people will always think what they want to believe. So, stop worrying about what other people will say and start making decisions based on what you want.

10. Read a motivational book. Reading encouraging material can make you feel better about yourself, which is a terrific method to boost your self-esteem.

Chapter 5: What is Chrometophobia and how to get over it?

Let's not pretend; debt and money may be really frightening. We live in a world where money practically has no bounds, so it's not a stretch to say that we've all experienced financial hardship at some time in our lives.

Chrometophobia: What is it?

Chrometophobia, sometimes known as chrematophobia, is concerned with everything related to concerns of money, including the fear of handling money, the dread of thinking about money, and the fear of spending money. The Greek words “Phobos”, which means "fear," and "chermato" which means "money," are combined to form chrematophobia, which is an excessive aversion to money.

Symptoms

Chrometophobia is an unnatural and irrational fear that has a wide range of symptoms with varying degrees of intensity. It is also less prevalent than other phobias, including acrophobia (the fear of heights) and claustrophobia (the dread of crowded places).

Extreme Reluctance to Consider Money

You may be bordering on chrometophobia if you find it difficult to develop a saving habit and avoid having to deal with unhealthy spending or feel unconcerned about it. Because you feel helpless to handle your finances or you're concerned you could run out of money, you can even stop saving money and making payments on your obligations.

Absence from activities

Your financial concerns may cause you to lose interest in your enjoyable hobby, forgo date night with your spouse, or forgo family movie night. When you have chrometophobia, you'll notice that you avoid your regular, delightful hobbies.

Want To Constantly Count Money

If you are continually counting the money in your wallet or logging into your bank account, you could have chrometophobia. If someone checked their bank account every day, wouldn't you suspect something was wrong?

Refusal to Handle Cash

If you continuously display resistance to touching money, you may have chrometophobia. It may be because the sight of money emotionally triggers you, or you may just be afraid of becoming sick from the germs on money.

Physical Illnesses or Depressive Thoughts

If your financial condition causes you to experience severe worry, it is advised that you speak with a mental health professional right away since chrometophobia may result in severe emotions of melancholy, anxiety, and hopelessness. Furthermore, it is advised that you get medical attention right away if you develop any of the physical signs of chrometophobia, such as shivering, nausea, dry mouth, or shortness of breath.

8 Typical Money phobias

1. Concern about losing one's job. Many people who worry about losing their means of subsistence end up in occupations they despise and are hindered in many other ways.

2. Reluctance to bargain for a wage increase. The worry and the fear of being threatened with termination or being let go may be rather overpowering for some individuals, despite the tremendous risk being well worth it.

3. Anxiety over running out of money. Many people live in constant fear that they will never be wealthy enough to support themselves.

4. Sensing loss financially. Many individuals have trouble figuring out what their major financial issues are, and they are unaware of their financial situation.

5. The anxiety of becoming a burden. I don't want to be a hassle for you. This phrase is typically spoken by those who are too concerned about burdening their family, spouse, or friends.

6. The worry that you will spend all of your money. Making money is not simple. Imagine losing every penny you worked so hard for. You did say, "God forbid," correct? Lol. That's it, indeed.

7. Apprehension about never paying off debt. Comparing your debt to your income in a system that so strongly promotes debt may be quite crippling, and the realization that you won't be able to escape your situation anytime soon can be extremely overwhelming.

8. Apprehension about using all your savings. Do you realize that some individuals would sooner go without food than waste their savings? When these individuals consider how long it took them to save up, the thought of squandering it all "just like that" might cause them to become frozen.

Psychological Techniques to Conquer Your Money Fear

1. Recognize your fear. Admitting that you have a fear is the first step toward overcoming it. With this, you'll be able to accept change rather than fight it and you may start your healing process.

2. Determine the root of your apprehension. Recognizing your concerns is OK, but why are you frightened in the first place? When you comprehend why you feel the way you do by locating the source of your fear, you'll be able to either remove the pressures or make changes.

3. Express your fear to others. It's concerning that so many people continue to avoid handling money issues and that anybody who discusses how much they spend or how much they make is seen as boastful and disrespectful. It's time we identified a professional, a colleague, a family, a friend, or a trustworthy partner with whom to discuss our challenges, aspirations, and worries while this society's money taboo persists. Start a conversation about money. Contrary to what society expects, act!

4. Do something to get over your fear. You may conquer your money phobias and progress on your financial journey with the aid of professional advice. When you engage with a professional like a therapist, mentor, or financial coach, you may develop a plan for recovery and you'll be able to recognize your weak spots as you become more aware of your money worries.

5. Be considerate of yourself. Being kind to yourself is the least you can do in a world when there is so much stress. Don't put yourself under extra strain while you navigate your finances, and be aware that negative self-talk might make you more frightened of money. So, while you examine your connection with money, keep in mind to be kind to yourself.

Chapter 6: Learning to Recognize and Overcome Your Fear of the Unknown

Because it is an inherent aspect of human existence, uncertainty is one of the problems we will face as we travel through life. What probably influences how you react to uncertainty is how terrified you are of the unknown. This explains why some individuals get emotionally immobilized by uncertainty while others flourish under such circumstances.

The psychiatric name for this kind of dread is "xenophobia," and in this case, what you don't actually know may damage you. You may also come to have an "intolerance of uncertainty," which is a state of mind in which confronted with an unexpected or unknown circumstance causes you to feel very agitated and frightened. You'll find some of the unclear situations in this situation to be quite intolerable.

Typical Symptoms

The physical impacts of fear are the same as the symptoms you go through when you have this phobia. they consist of heightened blood sugar (sugar) levels, fatigue, tense muscles, shallow breathing, and rapid heartbeat.

Be aware that if you are prone to worrying about the unknown, you can start to imagine the worst-case scenarios or develop the habit of catastrophizing, both of which might be harmful to your health.

Causes

Loss of predictability and Lack of control are the two main contributors to the dread of the unknown.

Inability To Predict

Since your anxiety level might increase when you can't make correct predictions due to a lack of knowledge, getting additional information is an excellent method to combat the lack of predictability.

No self-control

Have confidence in your ability to manage your own life. Your handicap and age might reduce your feeling of agency, and when you believe you have little control over your situation, your anxiety is likely to increase. To regain your feeling of agency, it is advised that you make a list of the things you can and cannot manage and examine your situation.

However, be aware that those who suffer from any of these issues, including depression, anxiety and fear disorders, alcohol use disorders, disordered eating, obsessive-compulsive disorder (OCD), and hoarding disorder, are more susceptible to this kind of anxiety.

How to Get Over Your Fear of the Unknown

1. **Challenge your presumptions.**

If you struggle with fear of the unknown, you need to look at your beliefs. Start by posing a few questions to yourself, such as:

- Do you feel constrained by cognitive distortions?

- Did you have to develop any cognitive distortions to get through previous challenges?
- How reasonable are your convictions?

2. Research your topic

If you have more knowledge, it will be simpler for you to make judgments. Growing your knowledge will give you more control over the situation, which is a terrific method to reduce your fear of the unknown.

3. Remain rooted in the present.

By taking one tiny action each day and listing the things you can manage, you may increase your feeling of control over your life and strengthen your sense of accountability. Taking action is a wonderful approach to lessen the likelihood of experiencing a bad consequence.

4. Maintain a healthy lifestyle to manage stress.

Here are some elements that may help you improve your capacity so that you can manage the tension that comes with uncertainty:

- Mindfulness
- Good Relationships
- Nutritious Food
- Exercise

5. Consult a reliable source.

Everybody needs a listening ear from time to time. There are a few useful techniques you may use to reframe your thought patterns, such as writing down your worries in a private notebook or speaking with a trusted friend. You can also process your fear of the unknown with the aid of a therapist.

Chapter 7: Silencing Inner Negativity and Taming Your Inner Critic

Your inner conversation has the power to either drive your success or keep you from realizing your full potential. As a result, you must learn to mute your inner critic. To have a more fruitful conversation with yourself and proactively deal with your negative ideas, you must also learn to control your inner critic.

1. Increase your awareness of your ideas. You have to realize that just because you think of something, it doesn't always indicate that it is true. Even if you become used to hearing your own narrations, pay attention to whatever you're thinking about and make an effort to be aware of the signals you're sending to yourself. Furthermore, be aware that our ideas often include exaggerations, biases, and disproportionate.

2. Stop thinking about it. Ruminating about your dubious or humiliating actions or statements won't help you find a solution to your situation. Even if there's a good possibility, that you'll be rehearsing your poor day or your error continually in your thoughts, you must realize that this behavior doesn't provide a fix. To avoid focusing on it, you may chat about anything else, arrange your desk, take a stroll, or engage in some other activity.

3. Consider the advice you would give your buddy if you were in his position. You know if you have a buddy who feels depressed after making a mistake or doing something wrong, you'll probably want to encourage him with motivating phrases like "it's not the end of the world" and the like. Now, offer yourself all the kind things that you would have spoken to your buddy.

4. Review the available evidence. Looking at bits of evidence from both sides can help you approach the subject less emotionally and more logically. Your critical ideas may sometimes be too pessimistic, but the facts you acquire and carefully consider can help you see reality more clearly.

5. Replace highly critical ideas with ones that are more truthful. When you have overly negative thinking, you should immediately respond with something more accurate. Instead of saying "I never do anything perfectly," you may add "at times, I do things incredibly well and occasionally I don't."

6. How horrible do you believe it would be if your beliefs were accurate? This is something you should contemplate. What would you really be feeling? The truth is that by constantly telling yourself that you can handle challenges or difficult circumstances, you may lessen the constant assault of unsettling ideas and boost your self-assurance.

7. Strike a balance between progress and acceptance. You see, nobody is flawless. Do not let anybody push you to be perfect. You will have some days when you do well and other days when you perform poorly. The only thing you can do is continue to be aware and strive to improve. Accept your shortcomings and make the decision to improve.

Chapter 8: Living a Courageous Life

The saying "there's no bravery without fear" is one you've definitely heard, and it's accurate because courage is the ability to react boldly when anxiety and concern are staring you in the face. It is erroneously interpreted to connect bravery with fearlessness since courage is acting in spite of the dread you experience. When you're brave, you'll be able to go for your goals in life, follow your aspirations, and take risks. If you've been battling with fear and you want to feel braver in your life, you may learn how to make the most of every circumstance and practice your courage in a variety of ways.

Advantages of Courage

Being brave involves acting in spite of the dread that unavoidably arises, weighing the benefits and dangers, and carefully considering your options. Overcoming your anxieties requires effort.

When you have greater bravery, you'll be able to do good things in your life and react effectively to hazards. You may have confidence in your talents when you have courage, and you can also pursue the things that are essential to you with more vigor.

Don't think you lack bravery if you sense fear, and don't allow this cause you to feel bad about yourself. One benefit of fear is that it causes you to slow down and carefully assess dangers, which is one of its positive effects. When you prepare yourself to confront your anxieties, you'll be ready to utilize a courageous-based reaction in lieu of your fear-based response. Without further ado, here are some further advantages of courage:

- When you embrace bravery and apply it to your life, you'll be able to feel happier all the time.
- When you're brave, you have a better chance of grabbing hold of chances when they come your way, are more likely to go after your ambitions, and end up being a more successful person.
- When you make the decision to be braver by venturing out of your comfort zone, you will be able to widen the experiences you have in your life and become a more well-rounded person.
- When you are bold, you will inspire others to follow your example.
- When you embrace bravery, you'll be able to see the world from a fresh viewpoint.

- Find your bravery if you've struggled with low self-esteem your whole life, and it will improve.

How to Be More Courageous in Your Life

1. Accept your weakness. If you're worried about others recognizing you for who you really are, be more open and vulnerable. Living from fear will leave you with little to no self-confidence, which is why you must embrace vulnerability.

2. Acknowledge your anxieties. As I previously said, nobody is naturally brave, therefore in order to conquer your fears and anxieties, you must first gather all the necessary knowledge about them. However, in order to do this, you must first be able to recognize your worries. Just as you open yourself up to others, you must acknowledge your worries.

3. Defeat your phobias. Exposing yourself to your anxieties is an excellent method to get over a fear or phobia. For instance, if you have a fear of cats, being friends with someone who owns a gorgeous cat may help you overcome your phobia and open your eyes to new perspectives.

4. Have an optimistic outlook. Every time you want to undertake something, stop focusing too much on what may go wrong. More importantly, let people adore you and express their passion for you; this is also a component of having a happy attitude. Do you know that when you behave as though you don't care about how other people feel about you, they term you a "hard guy"? Avoid making it your thing. If you don't do favors, love others shamelessly and let them do wonderful things for you.

5. Ease your tension. Everyone needs a rest. Enjoy your time off. Take pauses. Exercise. Be careful to eat healthily and get enough sleep. It's time to start prioritizing your health and taking part in hobbies or anything else that helps you relax since sometimes being exhausted is what causes you to feel afraid.

6. Exhibit bravery. Some individuals claim to enjoy "faking it till they make it," while others see this behavior as a display. So, whenever you get the opportunity, show bravery. If you notice someone in need, act bravely and step in or phone for assistance. Consider what you can do to assist rather than ignoring someone who is in danger. Being courageous is a powerful technique to face fear.

7. Recognize defeat but continue moving ahead. When you fail, don't curl up into a ball; keep pushing ahead. Move onward despite your shortcomings and let them carry you to the next level or stage. You gain experience the more times you fail. Failure itself isn't all that horrible, but when you allow it to get to you, it can be really hazardous and destructive.

8. Handle risk and unpredictability. Nothing in this life is certain or definite, therefore facing your worries by developing coping mechanisms is a fantastic approach to overcoming them. If you worry that you're about to lose a customer or your spouse to someone else, consider what you can do to retain them. Similarly, if you worry that your home will go into foreclosure, you can open an emergency savings account.

9. Continue learning. Never stop learning new things. Make sure to take advantage of any possibilities you come across to broaden your skill set or learn a new one. Develop your abilities, pick up new knowledge, and keep learning. When you are more knowledgeable and make sure you read everything you can about your industry, there will be less risk for you to take in order to succeed. You should also study the writings of eminent thinkers.

10. Recognize your obstacles. Being accountable becomes important at this point. Accept the challenges you face. Do you even realize that most of the time, fear is a mental state? Prepare yourself to face the challenges ahead rather than running away. Get yourself together to stay on the path even after you have faced your fears and challenges. Keep in mind that living will always put you ahead and that wasting time worrying will not help you at all.

Chapter 9: Jettisoning Your Fears: 7 Ways to Make Your Big Dream a Reality

1. Believe it. The first step to realizing your great desire is to believe it is feasible. Many people nowadays like pursuing goals they believe to be just out of reach or too huge for them, but little do they realize that the first step to achieving a big goal is simply believing in one's own potential.

2. Perform regular tasks. Although it is important to have faith, if you don't act on it, your faith will merely be passive. Your dreaming is worthless and useless if you don't do something about it. Start putting in some effort to go a little closer to your major ambition. No matter how little it seems, just keep going. Keep in mind that consistency is the key to winning. Additionally, you must take on everyday activities in order to realize your great ambition.

3. Assign a deadline to it. You must establish a deadline for achieving your big dream in order to continue moving forward and remain responsible. If you have a lofty goal but no specific deadline to meet, it will be difficult for you to maintain discipline. You could even become lethargic as a result since you'll always believe that "there's time." Keep in mind that if you don't have a deadline for anything, weeks, days, hours, minutes, and seconds might quickly slip your mind. As you start your trip, you may always establish particular dates to accomplish various milestones since time flies.

4. Have expansive, colorful dreams. Never allow what you see around you or what others say prevent you from pursuing your dreams. Make sure you have a clarity even after having large dreams, and constantly consider how it will make you feel when you realize that big dream you have been picturing.

5. Ignore the critics. There are some people in life who will support you when you start following your heart and chasing your dreams, and there are others who will discourage you and give you a thousand reasons why you shouldn't. People who constantly tell you that you can't do what you want to do need to be taught how to be ignored. Funny enough, these critics may include those close to your heart, like family or friends, as well as strangers who just have a passing familiarity with you. However, the argument still stands that you have what it takes to realize your desire since you are a special person. Don't let doubters hold you back from going for your great dream.

6. Tell other people about your dream. It's a good idea to share your dreams with people since you never know who you'll meet who can assist you in realizing them.

You're not doing well enough if you have a lofty ambition that you're hiding from the world. You may certainly attempt to be selective about the people you share your dreams with, but keep in mind that you are a special human with abilities that no one else has, like intelligence and initiative. Therefore, when you meet individuals and share your aspirations with them, some may be able to put you in touch with people who can help you obtain what you need to realize your dream. You may also meet people who will inspire, encourage, and lift you up when you are down.

7. Don't set high expectations. Don't have high expectations if you don't want to be let down and demotivated. Be prepared for obstacles on your trip and avoid being trapped by inflexible standards. Maintain momentum, think of things as inevitable, and create space for your great desire.

Chapter 10: Affirmations for Letting Go of Fear and Conquering Anxiety

When fear becomes crippling, it may really make our life difficult. Yes, to some extent, we all experience dread, and doing so may be challenging. We may use affirmations to strengthen our self-love, which will help us release fear and get over our fears. But it's not good to give into fear all the time.

Most of the time, one of the reasons we dread too much is because we don't love ourselves enough. Our self-confidence is also quite low, thus employing the effective method of positive affirmations is a straightforward approach to getting through some of our difficult circumstances. In the event that you decide to write your own positive affirmations, be sure to keep them upbeat, keep them in the present tense, be precise, and keep them succinct.

Without further ado, here are some inspiring quotes to help you face your fears:

- ✓ I learn from my errors. I am upbeat and self-assured; I accept the faults I've done.
- ✓ I like change because it spurs development in me.
- ✓ I am bravely living my life, and I feel empowered by facing my concerns.
- ✓ I let go of the hurt from my past.
- ✓ I am enthusiastic about my life, and I keep trying till I achieve.
- ✓ I have all the inspiration and drive I need to go after my ambitions.
- ✓ This brand-new day of possibility is a gift to me.

- ✓ Success is simple for me since I have all I need right now. I recognize my own value and am pleased of all my successes. I am gorgeous and full of strength.
- ✓ I am pushing through my fear and unquestionably defeating it. I have a bright future.
- ✓ Even if I may fight, it will still be worthwhile since I value my life and would do everything to protect it.
- ✓ I'm getting better, and I love myself just the way I am.
- ✓ I have the ability to alter my life, and even though I may be afraid, I will go through with it.
- ✓ I have access to mental clarity, I let go of any self-doubt, and my life is changing as I go on a quest to live a better one.

- ✓ I feel serene and at ease.
- ✓ I tenaciously and zealously defend my pleasure.
- ✓ I am never giving up because I am tenacious, and I deserve everything wonderful in life, including happiness, health, and prosperity.
- ✓ I have a lot to look forward to in my life.
- ✓ Because I have what it takes, overcoming my worries is simple.
- ✓ My dreams are worth battling for, and I will succeed, be happy, and thrive.
- ✓ The love I have for myself is unwavering, and I'm enjoying it.
- ✓ I believe in the course of life.

- ✓ I'm not flawless, therefore I'll refrain from judging myself, and if I have in the past, I'll let go of all the criticism.
- ✓ I am the universe's favorite, and the universe guards over me.
- ✓ Today, I'm living courageously.
- ✓ I have a lot of confidence and determination.
- ✓ I exhale my fear and I inhale my power.
- ✓ I'm finding it simpler and easier to go ahead without fear.
- ✓ All of my challenges are insignificant, and I'll definitely get beyond them.
- ✓ I'm grateful for how different I am.
- ✓ I'm giving it my all.

- ✓ I shall look toward the future with hope and pleasure.
- ✓ Anything I set my mind to; I can do. I am too energized and motivated to give up.
- ✓ I feel fortunate, loved, and supported; I let go of worry, anxiety, and fear.
- ✓ I trust and believe in myself.
- ✓ My skills are extraordinary and one-of-a-kind.
- ✓ If I really want to, I can do it.
- ✓ Life is always in my favor, and my self-assurance is escalating daily.
- ✓ I am physically able to complete my objectives.
- ✓ Thanks to all the challenges I face, I am continually developing.
- ✓ I'm more capable and resilient than I realize.

- ✓ When I concentrate on my thoughts, I may assist in making my dreams come true.
- ✓ Nothing that comes my way will be too much for me to manage.
- ✓ I'm courageous enough to take risks, therefore I can do that.
- ✓ No matter what occurs on the outside, I can be at peace inside because I am teaching myself to be full of wonder, delight, and curiosity.

Conclusion

You need to cope with your fear so that it won't hinder you in order to achieve your objectives in life and have a clear mind to start concentrating on the things that important to you in life. Some individuals may find that fear simply seems too typical, and if you agree with them and think that "fear is just fear" and decide not to work on your fear, the results might be disastrous. You shouldn't allow fear to rule your actions. You shouldn't let fear prevent you from achieving your goals and earning what you deserve.

How long will you continue to let fear influence your choices? It's high time you took control of the situation and demonstrated to your anxieties that you can scream far louder than they can. Decide to become a fearless person by taking control of your future and destiny. Keep in mind that the day you decide to face your fear head-on and look it in the eyes is the day you earn self-assurance, bravery, and strength.

www.ingramcontent.com/pod-product-compliance
Lightning Source LLC
LaVergne TN
LVHW050330160826
845677LV00014B/3579

* 9 7 9 8 8 4 8 3 3 2 5 8 2 *